Y0-CZQ-866

Out of This World

Space Stations

Brendan Bolton

Contents

ETA
Cuisenaire

Living in Space

Have you ever dreamed of being an astronaut?

Can you imagine speeding toward the stars in a space shuttle? Would you like to eat your food from a toothpaste tube? How about sleeping upright, strapped to a spacecraft wall so you don't float away? It sounds like fun, doesn't it?

But do you think you have the skills, fitness, patience, and courage to live and work in space? To become an **astronaut**, you need to study *hard*. All astronauts are specialists in a **field** of science or **engineering**, and many are also pilots.

Fitness is necessary, too, because only healthy people are chosen. Doctors don't do house calls in space! To live in space, you also need to be very patient, as astronauts live in extremely close quarters with fellow space travelers.

an astronaut exercising in space

Finally, you'll need courage, because life in space is more dangerous than you can imagine. Danger is every-where. **Space junk**, which can travel at speeds up to 17,000 miles per hour, can easily punch a hole in a spacecraft; or equipment could fail, leaving you without oxygen or stranded in outer space.

astronauts working together in cramped conditions

As you can see, living in space is no holiday...or is it? Find out with this book, as it explores life in space from the beginning of the space race to today.

Will a space vacation be possible in *your* lifetime?

an astronaut showering in space

The Space Race

Only sixty years ago, space travel was a distant dream. It was an idea explored in children's fantasies, science fiction novels, and radio plays. But, on February 24, 1949, the dream become reality when a *Bumper* rocket became the first engineered object to reach space.

The United States of America had obtained V-2 rockets from Germany at the end of the Second World War. These rockets, carrying explosives, had rained down on London during the war. The German rocket team and an American team worked together to launch the rocket to an **altitude** of 258 miles. The "space age" had begun.

the first U.S. space launch on January 31, 1958

The **superpowers**—the United States of America and the Union of Soviet Socialist Republics or **U.S.S.R.** (now known as Russia)—became locked in a race to be the first. These "firsts" included the first animal in space, the first man in space, the first woman in space, the first to land on the Moon, the first **satellite,** and the first space station.

Neil Armstrong was the first human being to walk on the Moon.

Billions of dollars (and **rubles**) were spent—and many lives lost—before each of these firsts became a reality. Progress in space travel and research became an issue of national pride. Politicians from both superpowers attached great importance to being the leader in space research.

Technological and scientific advances were jealously guarded secrets, so **espionage**, or spying, was often used to gain an advantage. There was some cooperation between the countries, but this was carefully limited by the U.S. and U.S.S.R. space agencies.

the *Bumper* rocket—the first engineered object to reach space

The Firsts

This timeline shows the first major events in outer space.

First	Mission	
Engineered object in space	*Bumper* rocket	1949
Satellite in orbit	*Sputnik 1*	1957
Animal in orbit (Laika the dog)	*Sputnik 2*	1957
Man in orbit (Yuri Gagarin)	*Vostok 1*	1961
Woman in orbit (Valentina Tereshkova)	*Vostok 6*	1963
Landing on the Moon	*Apollo 11*	1969
Space station	*Salyut 1*	1971
Space shuttle	*Columbia*	1981
Space station built from modules	*Mir*	1986
International space station	*ISS*	1998

Laika the dog—the first animal to orbit Earth

Yuri Gagarin was the first man in space.

Vostok 1 taking Yuri Gagarin up into space

Salyut 1—the first space station

Russian cosmonaut Valentina Tereshkova—the first woman in space

In 1952, Wernher von Braun, a German rocket scientist, first came up with the idea of creating a space station. His plan was for a eighty-three yard high, inflatable wheel-shaped station that would rotate to create artificial **gravity** for astronauts. It would be a permanent base in space for experiments, making observations, or launching new space missions.

An Early Attempt to Build a Space Station

Many people claim that the first space station in **orbit** was *Skylab*, but it was actually the second. The first space station was the U.S.S.R.'s *Salyut 1*, which was launched on April 19, 1971.

Little is publicly known about *Salyut 1*—perhaps because of its tragic end. Its primary mission was to study how space flight affected humans and to observe and photograph Earth from space. *Salyut 1* also contained a greenhouse to observe plant growth in space.

Salyut 1 over Paris

Salyut 1 was designed to hold a crew of three people. The crew was transported to the space station on a *Soyuz* spacecraft. The spacecraft attempted to **dock** with the space station on April 22, 1971, so the crew could board the station. This attempt failed as the hatch would not open.

In May 1971, a second crew didn't even make it to "lift-off." After finally taking off on June 6, a third crew succeeded in docking with *Salyut 1* on June 7, 1971. The three **cosmonauts** lived on the space station for twenty-four days.

Soyuz transported the crew to *Salyut 1*.

the three cosmonauts on *Salyut 1*

Soyuz spacecraft before docking with Salyut 1

On the return trip to Earth, the *Soyuz* spacecraft **depressurized**, killing all three crew members. The cosmonauts were not wearing **pressurized** spacesuits, as it was thought they were unnecessary. Now, all cosmonauts wear spacesuits on their **re-entry** flights.

The deaths of the three crew members prompted changes to the design of the *Soyuz* spacecraft. However, by the time the changes had been made, the space station was no longer usable. *Salyut 1* was **de-orbited** in October 1971, ending the six-month **mission**.

Skylab

The next attempt to establish a permanent human presence in space was the launch of *Skylab* on May 14, 1973. Launched by **NASA** from the Kennedy Space Center in Florida, it was boosted into the **atmosphere** using a *Saturn V* launch vehicle.

The launch was not without problems. As *Skylab* took off, vibrations caused a **meteorite** shield to rip off. The meteorite shield also damaged one of the craft's solar panels and covered another. Without power generated from the solar panels, life could not be supported on *Skylab*.

Scientists and engineers devised a plan to "roll" the craft, so that solar panels used to power a telescope could also be used to generate energy for the entire craft.

Unfortunately, the space station's position shift caused the temperature inside to increase to 125 degrees Farenheit. To decrease the temperature, a **parasol** sunshade (just like an umbrella) was constructed.

Saturn V launched *Skylab* and the successful *Apollo 11* mission to the Moon.

Now *Skylab* was ready for its first three-astronaut crew. The crew docked with *Skylab* on May 25, 1973. Their first task was to position the sunshade to lower the temperature to 74.8 degrees Farenheit. Once this was achieved, the crew could begin the **experiments** and observations that made up their mission. The first mission lasted twenty-eight days.

astronauts working on board a space station

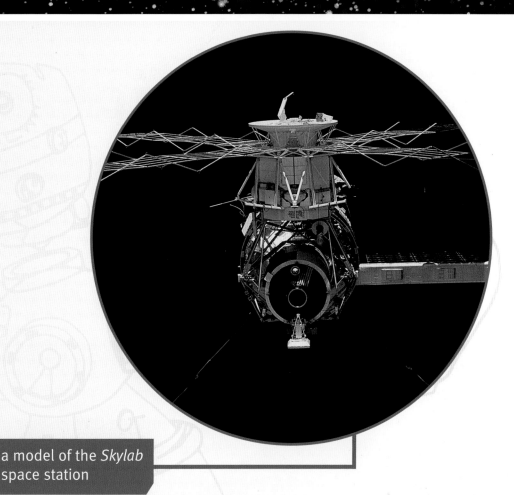

a model of the *Skylab* space station

Two more missions were undertaken, bringing the total time aboard *Skylab* to 171 days. The last crew returned to Earth on February 8, 1974.

After its final mission, *Skylab* was boosted into a stable position where it remained for the next ten years. However, all did not go according to plan. NASA soon decided that the craft was unstable. A controlled crash landing on Earth was the only solution.

In July 1979, *Skylab* returned to Earth in a fiery ball. Most of the debris landed in the Indian Ocean, but some parts crashed into the outback in Western Australia.

The Mir Space Station

Mir (a Russian word meaning "peace") was the next space station to orbit Earth. The Mir program began in 1986.

Mir differed from Skylab because it was not constructed on Earth and then launched into orbit. Instead, it was **assembled** in orbit from **modules** transported to space. Russian cargo vehicles were used to deliver many of the modules.

Although Mir was a Russian project, NASA space shuttles also transported some of the modules. These missions were a perfect example of the main purpose of the space shuttle program—a cargo plane for space.

But space shuttles didn't just deliver cargo to Mir. They also had a role as a passenger service, ferrying astronauts from all over the world to the space station.

SPACE STOP

The space shuttle: more fun than a bus!

Initially, *Mir* was designed to be used for only a few years. However, it was used as a space **laboratory** for fifteen years. During this time, over 125 astronauts from twelve countries lived aboard *Mir*.

the *Mir* space station in orbit

American and Russian crew members aboard space stations

Mir's Modules

Mir was the first space station to be assembled in space.
The diagram below shows the modules that made up *Mir*.

the *Mir* space station

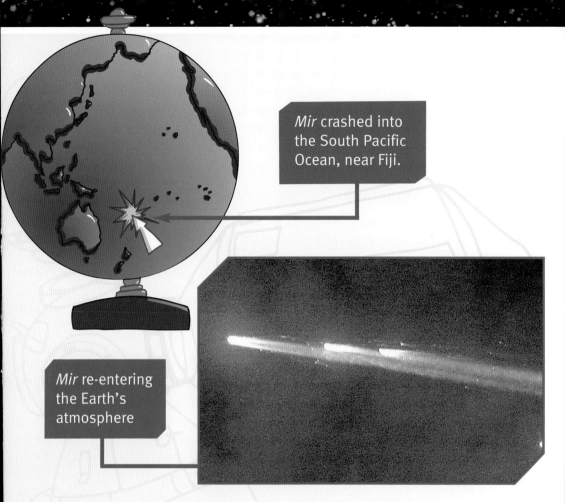

Mir crashed into the South Pacific Ocean, near Fiji.

Mir re-entering the Earth's atmosphere

In March 2001, the Russian space agency decided that *Mir* was no longer needed. Most of the modules that formed *Mir* were not designed to return to Earth. These modules would burn up as they entered the Earth's atmosphere. The parts that wouldn't burn up couldn't make a controlled landing and would crash.

To avoid damage to property or loss of life, *Mir* was moved into a position so that **debris** would splash down into the ocean in a **remote** area of the South Pacific. The remains of *Mir* re-entered Earth's atmosphere on March 23, 2001. As predicted, debris landed near Fiji. The world watched closely through numerous media reports.

International Space Station

After fifty years of the space race, the world's space agencies finally decided to work together in the late 1990s. The result is the *International Space Station*, or *ISS*. The first of its fourteen sections was launched in 1998. The *ISS* is due for completion in 2006.

NASA's space shuttles and Russia's *Soyuz*, *Proton*, and *Progress* rockets will take part in over forty missions to complete the space station.

Laboratories, power **generation** modules, and living quarters will be added over an eight-year period. Astronauts will participate in activities outside the space station.

When the *International Space Station* is fully operational, it will have living quarters for up to seven astronauts. However, only three astronauts will be on board at one time.

Sixteen countries are involved in the construction and operation of *ISS*. These are the United States, Russia, Canada, Japan, the European Space Agency (eleven countries), and Brazil.

a model of the *International Space Station*

Space Tourists

Do you want to travel into space to see what it's really like? If you have millions of dollars to spare, you can!

The first paying space tourist was sixty-year-old American businessman, Dennis Tito. He reportedly paid $20 million to the Russian Space Agency to take him 250 miles into space. Lift-off for Dennis's space vacation was May 1, 2001. He spent eight days aboard the *International Space Station* before returning to Earth on May 9.

Dennis is not unfamiliar with space, as he studied **aeronautics** and engineering before joining NASA's Jet **Propulsion** Laboratory in 1964. He worked with NASA until 1972.

While aboard the space station, Dennis found time for more than sightseeing. He helped to prepare food for the astronauts, took photographs, and filmed the Earth.

space tourist Dennis Tito just before lift-off

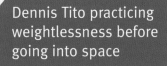

Dennis Tito is not the only "non-astronaut" to visit space. Prior to the 1986 explosion that destroyed the *Challenger* space shuttle, NASA shuttle passengers included two American politicians. A Japanese television network sent a journalist to *Mir* for a week in 1990. The following year, a British chemist, Helen Sharman, also visited.

Chances are, Dennis Tito won't be the last space tourist.

Would you like to be a space tourist?

Will you be next?

Glossary

aeronautics   the study of flight, particularly related to aircraft

altitude   the height of anything, such as a mountain or a building, especially above sea level

assembled   fitted or joined together

astronaut   a person trained for traveling in space

atmosphere   the mixture of gases surrounding Earth, a star, or a planet

billion   one thousand million (1,000,000,000)

cosmonaut   a Russian astronaut (*see* astronaut)

debris   the pieces of something that is broken

de-orbited   left orbit (*see* re-entry)

depressurized   lost pressure (*see* pressurized)

dock   to link together in orbit

engineering   an area of work that involves designing, building, and maintaining objects such as engines, cars, bridges, and machines

espionage   using spies to find secret information

experiments   tests to show that something is true, to examine an idea, or to find out something you don't know

field   an area

generation   the process of making power

gravity   a force that pulls things toward Earth

laboratory   a room used for carrying out scientific experiments

meteorite   a rock-like object that is left when a planet or a star explodes; this debris can fall to Earth

mission   when spacecraft are sent to space to achieve a particular task

modules   separate units that together can make up a whole, such as a spacecraft

NASA   National Aeronautic and Space Administration

orbit   the curved path followed by a planet or satellite as it moves around a planet or star

parasol   an umbrella to protect people or things from the sun

pressurized   maintaining normal air pressure in an enclosed space, such as inside a spacecraft

propulsion   power that moves something forward

re-entry   the point at which a spacecraft returns to the Earth's atmosphere

remote   distant

ruble   Russian currency

satellite   an object orbiting around a planet or star

space junk   parts of old spacecraft in orbit

superpowers   a term used to describe the two most powerful countries on Earth between 1945 and 1990 (U.S.A. and U.S.S.R.)

technological   using science to assist industry or commerce

U.S.S.R.   Union of Soviet Socialist Republics

Index